Multiple Sclerosis, Muscular Dystrophy & A L S

©1993

Kurt W. Donsbach, D.C., N.D., Ph.D.
H. Rudolph Alsleben, M.D., D.O., Ph.D.

TABLE OF CONTENTS

TABLE OF CONTENTS (cont.)

MULTIPLE SCLEROSIS

WHAT IS MULTIPLE SCLEROSIS?

Multiple Sclerosis (MS) is a disease that effects the white part or myelin sheath of the central nervous system. This may affect anywhere from the brain stem downward. The problems of MS begin when a type of cholesterol forms in the myelin sheath which surrounds the nerve. As the plaque enlarges, the normal nerve transmission from the brain is interrupted as it travels from the brain to the muscles which control some bodily function. The result is a sudden and mysterious inability of the patient to perform some task which is normal.

Typical early MS symptoms are an unstable, unsteady walk, blurred vision, or double vision in one or both eyes, sudden numbness in the extremities, slurring of speech, loss of bladder and/or bowel control are all symptomatic. Any combination of these may be present in any single individual, but there is no diagnostic certainty, particularly in the beginning.

Let it be understood that there is usually a blood, urine or x-ray test that can be used by a physician to diagnose most diseases. Not so with MS, often the doctor suspects the problem but has no definite criteria for a positive diagnosis in the beginning. As the disease progresses, the diagnosis becomes much more apparent and the physician has the unpleasant task of telling the patient that they are the victim of one of the real mysteries of medicine for which there is no cure and not even a positive form of palliative therapy.

Of all the diseases which present themselves to a doctor, those of the nervous system are by far the most difficult to treat. In MS, the nerve impulse which controls the function of specific muscles in a most ingenious and not totally understood way, is literally "short-circuited." The message from the brain just simply does not arrive at its intended destination because it got "derailed" somewhere along the path where a deterioration of the insulating fiber (the myelin sheath) of the nerve allowed it to go astray.

WHY?

The $64,000 question has to be: Why does a form of cholesterol (remember that cholesterol is an integral part of the myelin sheath) literally choke the life out of the myelin sheath and cause this disease? No one really knows. There are several theories that have some strong advocates, but believe me - at this point in time, no one can prove their theory. Let's take a look at some of the more prominent.

Auto-Immune Theory This is based upon the known fact that under certain circumstances, the body mistakes certain parts of itself as an intruder and proceeds to attack itself. This is also thought to be true in rheumatoid arthritis and lupus erythematosis. It gets very muddy when you consider that we can see the "bad" cholesterol in the nerve of Multiple Sclerosis patients on autopsy. It doesn't make sense that the immune system would send cholesterol to do its' job.

Genetic Predisposition Statistically, people who have close relatives with MS are 5 to 20 times more likely to get the disease than the general population. This is a pretty strong link, since it makes sense with what we now know about inherited genetic strengths and weaknesses. A recessive or weak gene, which could be used to substantiate this theory, has not been found by anyone up to this date.

Chemical Theory This would fit in with certain findings that an unexpected epidemic of MS will break out in certain areas, without any pattern as to families. One such incidence occurred in a small community which, by all national averages should not have had more than one case of MS, and yet seven cases occurred within five years. However, none of these incidents came up with a causative chemical, nor has any particular substance ever been isolated in a majority of victims.

Virus Theory Not isolated, never identified, the viral theory of MS causation intrigues me the most. It has no more proof than any of the others, yet it makes sense to me. A reclusive virus, which may inhabit a large number of individuals, may, under the right circumstances, explosively multiply and cause the deterioration of the myelin sheath. We know that many viruses love to hide in the nervous system - the herpes virus is a good example. As stress triggers some of these other viruses, it could also trigger this "phantom." There seems to be a very strong relationship between stress and the incidence of MS. Most, but not all, MS patients can identify a heavy period of stress just before their first symptoms broke out. They usually can pinpoint relapses as occurring shortly after heavy bouts of emotional stress. MS also is a great "ebb and flow" disease. Symptoms can be very heavy for a period and then fade away, sometimes almost totally for periods of months or even years, only to return with a vengeance. That would also fit in with a viral theory of causation. The biggest flaw in this theory is the presence of cholesterol plaques in the myelin sheath. Maybe a combination of the viral theory and the next one I will mention will give us an even better working model.

Drs. Swank and Horrobin Theory I have taken the liberty of combining the work that these two researchers have accomplished, because they are both parallel and complimentary. Dr. Swank is one of the most respected individuals in MS research. His theory revolves around the fact that there is a definite difference in the fat content of MS patients' myelin sheath and that of non-MS individuals. He believes that the blood platelets become sticky from the mal-utilization of ingested fats and literally plug up some of the small capillaries which feed the myelin sheath. The cells then die of starvation and toxic waste accumulation. Cholesterol plaque formation is rather easily explained in this scenario. Dr. Horrobin contends that an imbalance of prostaglandins exists which causes the body to damage the myelin sheath. Prostaglandins are hormone-like chemicals manufactured in the body from essential fatty acids. When there is an imbalance or an inadequate amount of essential fatty acids, these prostaglandins are not made in adequate amounts. Another factor is the ingestion of too many trans-fatty acids, such as those found in margarine, shortenings and other hydrogenated products. These trans-fatty acids interfere with the enzymes necessary to manufacture prostaglandins.

Donsbach Theory I thought it might be okay to give my theory, since you don't have to prove a theory right away, and no one else has proven theirs, and I'm basing mine on some of theirs, along with some clinical experience and common sense. As I indicated, I believe that there is very likely a viral factor in the etiology of MS. The ebb and flow, the aggravation by stress are extremely characteristic; and the anti-viral treatment that I have given MS patients has been more than accidentally successful, even though we haven't had enough years follow through to give long term statistics.

In addition, I believe that there is a fat discrepancy in the MS patient. Let us take a look at a program of diet manipulation that Dr. Swank used for over twenty years and followed patients progress carefully. The work which Dr. Swank did has been carefully and religiously ignored by the entire medical profession, as well as the National Multiple Sclerosis Society; a kind of "shunning" that often takes place in the field of health services toward any answer to a problem that does not fit into the "chemical" or "surgical" domain.

THE DR. SWANK LOW FAT PROGRAM

In order to understand Dr. Swank's program, you should be aware of his rationale in formulating it. There is a significant statistical correlation between northern climates and MS. People living in Minnesota have approximately 60 cases of MS per 100,000 population. In Louisiana, there are less than 6 cases per 100,000. Holland has one of the highest incidences of the disease in the world, as well as Norway. Westerners (Europeans and North Americans) have a much higher rate of the disease than do Asians, Orientals, Africans, South Americans, etc.

The thread that Dr. Swank felt was significant was the dietary influence on those in cold climates as compared to those in warmer zones. An even closer look at this factor indicated that even in those high incidence areas such as Norway, where the dietary fat intake was primarily that of fish, the incidence became much lower than those eating less fish.

Is there a protective factor in fish? Is there a negative factor in other fats, such as butter? These questions are not fully answered, even with the Swank Diet, which I will outline, but we can make some assumptions, which I will do after the outline. To put all of this in its proper perspective, you must recognize that so many factors enter into a disease like MS, even when statistics such as those I have just quoted are put forth, the "other" factors which we are not addressing may be as important as those which we are concerned with. As an example, there are many instances in medical history in which a therapy or treatment was successful in practice - but not because of the reason put forth by the originator of the therapy. So the Swank theory of MS treatment seems to be quite effective, as we shall see, but not necessarily for the reasons which he assigns.

Dr. Swank was the head of the department of Neurology of the University of Oregon Medical School in Portland, Oregon. He wrote a book entitled, "The Multiple Sclerosis Diet Book," which is still available. His diet is quite specific in restriction of fat intake - all fat intake such as meat fat, butter, margarine, shortenings, milk, cheese, etc. The diet is based upon his conclusions that all saturated fat is bad for the MS patient and must be severely restricted.

In actual practice, he must have something. Dr. Swank published a paper on 146 patients who had followed his program for more than twenty years. It is true that only a few actually improved but, in MS, the rule is you always eventually get worse! So no progression of the disease is remarkable progress. As a comparison: after 10 years on the Swank diet, 25% of the patients could not work or walk, while after the same period of time on a program from the Mayo clinic, which did not include any dietary modifications, 50% could not work or walk. Mortality numbers were even more startling. After 15 years of the Swank protocol, only 6% of the patients had died, 24% of the control group had passed away. After 30 years, 18% of the Swank group had passed away, 63% of the non-diet patients had expired. The only basic difference in the two programs was the Swank patients were on a very low fat diet.

The Dr. Swank program allows only the equivalent of 6 teaspoons of "hard fat" per day. Two ounces of red meat, completely trimmed of all fat, equals one teaspoon of "hard fat." Any reader of this who is interested in following the Swank diet religiously should buy Dr. Swank's book with all the specific recipes and food suggestions in order to be able to easily recognize the many ways "hard fats" are disguised in modern foods. In addition, Dr. Swank does recommend some oil daily, including cod liver oil. This is rich in eicosapentanoic acid (EPA) and docosohexanoic acid (DHEA) which are essential fatty acids of the omega three variety. In conjunction with the omega six fatty acids, the omega three essential fatty acids are extremely important in the prostaglandins, which Dr. Horrobin talks about.

If we put these parts together, we may be able to formulate a concept that would explain the results that Dr. Swank's program achieved. It may also lead us to the remarkable success that another doctor has had in treating MS - Dr. Hans Neiper of Germany. When I put these concepts together, I saw miracles happening!

DR. HANS NEIPER

In Hanover, West Germany resides a real medical innovator, a man who was not content to "follow the leader" in medicine, one who was willing to practice as his conscience dictated and experience taught him. Dr. Hans Neiper has clinical records of over 1,500 MS patients that he has treated over a period of twenty years. These records indicate a marvelous chronic remission (lack of symptoms) rate in a disease which, according to the medical profession and the Multiple Sclerosis Foundation, cannot be helped.

In return for his findings, and for helping hundreds of "incurable" patients, Dr. Neiper has been accused of charlatanism and fraud by medical brethren, particularly those in the U.S. He supposedly "lures" the hopeless MS patient to Germany, where most of them seem to have spontaneous remissions, which would have occurred anyway. The amazing thing is that most of the remissions remain permanently, at least as long as the patient stays on his protocol.

His patient waiting list is almost six months, since he has limited facilities and can only see a restricted number of patients daily. If his treatment was not successful, he surely would not be busy after twenty years of endeavor. The word would be out and patients just wouldn't come. The opposite is true, and he has been gracious enough to write and lecture on his concepts of cause and treatment so that other physicians who are interested may benefit.

CALCIUM EAP

One of the mainstays of the Neiper program is a substance called Calcium EAP. This is a normal substance in the human body, which had not been assigned a function, but it was definitely present, particularly as calamine phosphate. Dr. Neiper assigns the function of cell membrane protector to this substance and assumes that it is in short supply in MS patients because when he supplements it, they get better. When such supplementation is stopped, they have flareups of symptoms, which are relieved when Calcium EAP is reinstated.

However, as natural as calcium is, and calamine phosphate is, the FDA takes the position that it is a drug. In fact, one which has not been approved, therefore, unavailable by any means to the patient who might be improved by its use. We supply Calcium EAP to innumerable MS patients from our hospital in Mexico because it is unavailable in the U.S.

In treating the MS patient during their first stay, we use the Calcium EAP by infusion or "push" directly into the vein. After one or two such injections, most patients feel better and symptoms begin to subside.

Other products included in the Neiper protocol include calcium and magnesium orotate, potassium, and Calcium EAP, all in tablets which constitute the long term therapy that the patient follows after they leave the hospital. You can be sure that once the light is turned on, these people want to stay that way.

FITTING IT IN

The Neiper protocol and theories fit in well because he

says the Calcium EAP is a cell membrane protector. Regardless if you subscribe to the auto-immune theory, or the virus theory, or the improper fat metabolism theory, the substance which helps all of them (Calcium EAP) fits in with all because it is a cell membrane protector.

These then, are the major concepts which are out as to the etiology of MS. There are other substances that have been found to be particularly helpful in cases of this disease, some of them without any other therapy, including Calcium EAP, being instigated.

OCTOCOSANOL

Carlton Fredericks, more than anyone, made us aware of a special fat soluble component of wheat germ oil which has a beneficial effect on nerves and nervous system related disorders. Octocosanol is said to be responsible for the awakening of individuals who have been in lengthy comatose circumstances, to have aided those who had strokes recover impaired function more quickly than normal, and as a single substance, to benefit the MS victim immeasurably. There hasn't been a lot of fanfare for this substance but, we feel it is important enough to utilize it for every MS patient that we see. Rather high dosages are given, particularly in the beginning of therapy.

SNAKE VENOM

I have been accused of being a snake oil salesman for many years because I reported on the use of "alternative" medicines. It seems almost poetic justice that I should find snake venom of benefit for some of our patients. The research is quite voluminous on this substance, which is carefully gathered and processed. The normal method of use is to inject one half cc under the skin every day, or every other day, or at longer intervals.

The miraculous return of control over bladder and bowel function, which often occurs rapidly after beginning therapy, is most rewarding indeed. I have used this substance also for pain relief and in certain forms of arthritis with excellent results. The mechanism is probably similar to a vaccine in that it stimulates a responsive function in the body which overcomes that which was causing the symptoms.

I once had a patient who had been stung over 1,500 times by bees in order to help his arthritis. He had a temporary subsiding of symptoms from these repeated bee stings, which probably worked in a similar way to the snake venom which we use. As I said, medicine uses this principle in making vaccines to stimulate our immune system.

Unfortunately, only one company still continues to make the snake venom and, unless there is an increased use, they will probably be put in a position of closing because of lack of interest.

HOW THE VENOM WORKS

Without being technical, the particular snake venom used in MS has two main actions. One of them is based upon the viral theory of causation. When the venom is injected into the body, it enters the cell in minute amounts and does not allow any other type of virus to invade that cell because the receptor sites on the cell have been blocked. In order to understand this a bit more easily, think of it this way - when one is infected with one virus, be it measles, chicken pox, etc., you do not get infected with another virus at the same time.

Previous experience with polio virus has demonstrated that sub-lethal doses of the snake venom injected into monkeys 24 hours following the inoculation of those monkeys with the polio virus could prevent the onset of the disease. Theoretically, the venom, because of its extreme rapidity of dispersement, took up all the receptor sites in the cells and prevented the polio virus from finding a home.

The other major benefit of the venom is its nerve re-growth factor and its muscle toning effect. A demonstrated nerve response after venom injection led neuroscientists to refer to the effect as that of a "jumper cable" on impaired nerves. The benefit of this to the MS victim is obvious. Researchers of the venom therapy say: "We do not know whether the ability of some non-ambulatory patients to become ambulatory is a result of symptomatic relief due to improved nerve conduction induced by the nerve re-growth factors, or the result of the action of the venom on the disease process itself. It is possible that the nerve growth factor plays an important part in this, especially in patients who demonstrate a gradual, continuing improvement in their mobility. We believe that this fraction or group of fractions is responsible for improved atonic bladder control, increased sensitivity of the feeling in the extremities and greater stamina."

Can snake venom be tolerated by everyone? That questions comes up because of the report that someone, somewhere, died of anaphylactic shock from its use. We use extremely minute test doses for two days before we begin the regular injections (which are only 1/10 cc) and have never had anyone show an allergic reaction or have a problem.

But don't get the idea that snake venom is the total answer to MS. Tests have indicated that 33% of the patients which use it have excellent results, 66% have some improvements, 1% have no benefits, **but 0% deteriorated while on the therapy!** This in itself is a miracle because eventually everyone with MS deteriorates. The rule of thumb is that when you go into remission after an "exacerbation," you really don't have much left. Like the Neiper therapy, snake venom users seem to hold their own at worst, and most of them get better. **That's why we use both!**

GLA (Gamma Linoleic Acid)

Linoleic acid, a polyunsaturate which is the main essential fatty acid in the diet, tends to be low in the blood of MS patients and to tends fall further during the "exacerbation" periods. From this information, which has been well researched and documented, a double blind test was set up with 87 patients being treated with linoleic acid and 85 controls not receiving it. The test period was two and one half years. The results were quite demonstrative.

1. Treated patients with limited disability at entry had a smaller increase in disability than did controls.
2. Treatment reduced the severity and duration of relapses at all levels of disability for all those treated with linoleic acid.

Dr. Horrobin, an advocate of this kind of therapy, was somewhat critical, in that he felt the dosages given were inadequate for the patients and even better results would have occurred if the dosages were higher.

The body does not use linoleic acid as such, it breaks it down to GLA (gamma linoleic acid) and then further to prostaglandins. Rather than using the crude oils which contain linoleic acid, most doctors now are using GLA concentrate which is available in both capsule and tablet form. All of our patients receive daily dosages of GLA and are maintained for long periods of time on this substance.

STRESS

I need to spend some time on the effect of stress on this disease. It has been made extremely apparent that the ebb and flow of this disease is directly related to the amount of stress in the life of the patient. If there is one thing that is constant in the detailed history we take with this type of patient, it is the heavy stress that exists. Because of this, we have devised a program for our patients to learn how to "de-stress" themselves. We have a chamber utilizing lights and subliminal suggestion set in music conducive to clearing the brain of conflicting emotions. When they go home, they can take a copy of this tape with them and recreate the inner tranquility that is so important to them.

The subject of subliminal suggestion as a healing tool is very much in the news today. We have found it of assistance in many diseases, since it is becoming more and more apparent that stress causes certain organs and glands to go on hyper-function, but at the same time puts our entire healing forces into neutral.

Subliminal suggestion, with the proper mood music and sounds, can create a desirable internal environment that is conducive to healing our physical body. An hour spent in this way every day can enhance your quality of life manyfold.

WHAT PATIENTS SAY

"I am 48 years old and have MS. I was diagnosed in 1970 and was able to continue working, off and on, until 1977 when I was forced to retire at age 45. Since that time, I was getting progressively worse after trying conventional drugs. I am now able to walk with a walker (before I was confined to a wheelchair most of the time). I now have excellent bladder control. This was a constant embarrassment for me before treatment."

"All my bladder symptoms have been reversed since the 2nd day of the injections. I was having retention, with residual urine and overflow problems. I can now void freely. I am most grateful!"

"I can now stand upright more easily and do not have to hold on to the walls and furniture like I used to. Although I use a cane, now it serves more as a light guide rather than a support."

"When I came to Hospital Santa Monica, I wobbled like a drunken sailor, and needed two canes to be mobile at all. I could hardly be understood by others because of slurred speech. I could not, under any circumstances, carry or balance anything in my hands or arms. When I left, I was walking without wobbling and without canes; my speech had improved to where people could understand me, and I was easily carrying my food trays in the dining room. Thank you, thank you for making my life worth living. I am now back at work, before I sat at home and contemplated suicide. You saved my life."

"I look healthier, feel better, ambulate better, can tolerate the pain, even have sense of well being, which I certainly did not have before. I don't use a wheelchair at all - don't need a walker even! My appetite has improved, and I certainly have more strength. Last, but not least, I had been wearing glasses because of nerve degeneration, I am now reading small print most of the time without glasses. Those nerve shots sure did the trick for me."

These are some of the many letters we have on file from patients who have undergone the MS protocol at our facility. This protocol is not married to any single factor, we instead use a blend of the Neiper program, the Swank low fat diet, snake venom therapy, hydrogen peroxide infusions, and the reintroduction to the diet of specific nutritional factors, including the omega six fatty acids and octocosanol. To the best of my knowledge, our program is the only program which coordinates the entire spectrum of known knowledge in the treatment of MS. It has been extremely rewarding from an emotional standpoint to witness the results exhibited by patients like those whom we have quoted above.

The Donsbach Protocol

Please understand that, although I call this the Donsbach Protocol, it is a combination of many other very brilliant people's work. I feel my contribution is the common sense combination of proven therapies. For reasons beyond my comprehension, the Multiple Sclerosis Society and the medical profession as a whole have ignored the true plight of the MS victim and literally leave them to fend for themselves. The party line is that there is no help for MS, **therefore please do not try anything, even though literature abounds with success stories for several different therapies.**

This response is based upon the rationale that "it hasn't been tested with double blind studies." Those words are lies, because much of what I have reported here is the result of double blind or at least controlled studies. If you have MS - **you can be helped!** Please note, I did not say "cured", but if you can restore some function, or if you are in the beginning stages, or if you can be put into permanent remission, isn't that a significant benefit? Here is the protocol.

Neiper Supplements - All patients get the EAP injections and tablets, as well as all the other Neiper recommendations, which includes a restriction of Vitamin C as a supplement.

Swank Low Fat Diet - This restricted program allows a total of 6 full teaspoons of fat or oil in your diet daily.

This requires the careful trimming of all fat from meats, removal of skin from chicken, reduction in sources of oils such as salad dressings, etc. The great results that this diet alone produced are enough to convince me of its value.

Snake Venom Therapy - These minute injections are a bit uncomfortable to some at first, but when the results become evident, all concur that it was worth it. The possibility of nerve re-growth, although not proven, is the only explanation for some of the remarkable function restorations we see. For those who need it, we teach them to give this to themselves at home.

Hydrogen Peroxide Infusions - In conjunction with other anti-virals, I use a diluted solution of 35% food grade hydrogen peroxide as an anti-viral and tissue oxygen enhancer. (You can read more about this in my book on the subject of oxygen.)

GLA - The omega six fatty acid known as gamma linoleic acid has been thoroughly researched by Dr. Horrobin as to its effects on MS, All our patients receive this as a daily addition to their diet. I also add a specially processed flax seed oil to the daily diet, since it is one of the richest sources of GLA.

Octocosanol - This wheat germ oil concentrate is an incredibly valuable food for the nervous system. It should not be confused with wheat germ oil, as only a small fraction of the mother oil is octocosanol. We use a rather heavy dosage of this on a daily basis for the MS

24

patient.

Amantadine - This has been the most successful anti-viral I have found that works with the MS patient. It has an effect all alone which would lead one to support the viral theory of causation of this disease, but the effect is not necessarily what we would expect. The patient usually feels more energy, complains less of fatigue than usual. This could be because of viral containment, but could also result from some other benefit that we don't understand. It is not unusual for medications to give us effects other than those for which they were originally designed. But, since it has a beneficial effect, and it doesn't have side effects, I am happy to include amantadine in our protocol.

DeStressing - We have discussed at length the relationship of stress and the exacerbation of the symptoms of MS. Our approach is to use controlled lighting, audible and subliminal suggestions in both audio and video cassette form in a special booth designed for maximum relaxation. The cassettes can be purchased to use at home. At the present time, I am designing a personal chamber that could be used in your home which would give you all of these factors, the lights, the audio and video, in an affordable module. It will be applicable to other diseases as well, if combined with the proper audio and visual aids.

Supplements - This will always be an area of controversy, because of the many different theories as to what is beneficial and what is potentially harmful. I have followed the Dr. Neiper admonition to limit the Vitamin

C for MS patients and recommend the following supplements:

> Oral Chelating Formula - 2 tablets with each meal
> Vitamin E 400 - 1 capsule with each meal
> Free Amino Acid Complex - 2 tablets with each meal
> Oat Bran Wafer - Chew 6 or 8 daily
> Flax Seed Oil - 2 Tblsp. at breakfast & dinner
> Octocosanol - 2 capsules with each meal
> GLA - 2 capsules with each meal
> Neiper Supplements - (4) 1 of each with each meal

I know this amounts to 13 tablets and capsules with each meal. Many complain that there can't be any room left for food. But, the long term benefits usually convince even the most vocal protesters. We package the entire supplements into baggies for breakfast, lunch and dinner, making it convenient and relieving the patient of the biggest burden of all - that of trying to have everything necessary on hand at all times. It is packaged into monthly increments, so you always have the entire supplement protocol.

References

Multiple Sclerosis: Twenty Years on Low Fat Diet, R.L. Swank Arch. Neurology 23:460-74, 1970

Treatment of Multiple Sclerosis with Nicotinic Acid and Thiamin M.T. Moore Arch. Int. Med. 65:18, 1940

Multiple Sclerosis: Vitamin D and Calcium as Environmental Determinants of Prevalence P. Goldberg Intern. J. Environ. Stud. 6-19-27 & 121-29, 1974

Essential Fatty Acids: M. Alter et al Arch. Neurol 31:267, 1970

J.M. French Br. J. Clinical Prac. 31:117-21, 1984

S. Gul et al. J. Neurol, Neurosurg, Psychiat, 33:506, 1970

B. Gerstl et al, Brain, 84:310, 1961

H. Mertin & C.J. Meade Brit. Med. Bull. 33:67-71, 1977

H. Sanders et al J. Neurol, Neurosurg. Psych., 31:321-5, 1968

R.H.S. Thompson Pro. Roy. Soc. Med. 59:269, 1966

Multiple Sclerosis: The Rational Basis for Treatment with Evening Primrose Oil, D. Horrobin, Med. Hypotheses 5:365-78, 1979

Dietary Supplementation with Efamol and Multiple Sclerosis, L.O. Simpson et al. New Zea. Med. Journ. 98(792): 1053-54, 1985

New Treatment for Multiple Sclerosis, A. Winter Neurol. & Orthoped. J. of Med. & Surg. 5:1, April 1984

Pyridoxine and Thiamine Therapy in Disorders of the Nervous System, S. Stone, Dis. Nerv. Sys., 11:131-38, 1950

Research on Multiple Sclerosis, C.W.M. Adams, Thomas Publ. III, 1972

Mechanism of Action of Nerve Growth Factor and its Antibodies, K. Harper & H. Thoenen, Ann. Rev. of Pharm. & Tox., 21:205-29, 1981

The prior pages of discourse on Multiple Sclerosis were written by Dr. Donsbach. The next pages were written independently by Dr. Alsleben. It is interesting to see how these two parallel their thinking but express themselves in different ways. You will benefit by absorbing both of these wholistic healers wisdom.

Multiple Sclerosis

Multiple Sclerosis is a form of brain and nerve damage. Judging from the nature of the change and its possible causative agents, it is likely that every person has a certain amount of this problem present in the nervous system. How much you have determines whether you know that you have it.

The degenerations are probably the same no matter where they occur. They just change their names to match their locations. In other words, Multiple Sclerosis, Lateral Sclerosis, Dermal Sclerosis, Nephrosclerosis and Arteriosclerosis are all the same pathology. They are just occurring at different locations.

In this lecture, we will study Multiple Sclerosis as an example of the neuro-dystrophic process.

Visualize this picture. A patient rolls down the corridor of the office in a wheelchair. She is paralyzed from the waist down. The patient is without feeling and without the ability to move her legs. She describes her disease to me and her history goes fifteen years into the past, to the age of fifteen. Her first recollections were of a slight ache in an ankle. She remembered that she had what she thought was a head cold that left her a little dizzy but, in a week, it went away. She remembered not being able to focus her eyes sharply on close objects but, by the time she went to the eye doctor, it was gone. Today, the patient is totally disabled, paralyzed and confined to a bed or wheelchair. Fifteen years ago, her problem was only a little cold or something.

Here is a questions. When did her disease, now called Multiple Sclerosis, begin? Did it begin when she was confined to a wheelchair as a paralyzed wreck? Or did it begin many years ago when flu-like symptoms were occurring with more than usual frequency?

For fifteen years there was no treatment known and therefore, none administered. She was finally diagnosed as a Multiple Sclerotic and you know what that is - it is a non-treatable, incurable disease.

Today, in just three treatments, she has experienced a return of sensation in the legs, ability to move both legs and the capability of leaving the wheel chair for awkward, but unassisted, strolls of five or ten feet. How is this possible in a so-called incurable disease?

Multiple Sclerosis, as we know it today, did not exist prior to the 20th century and it was not until the period following the First World War that it became a disease to be dealt with in this country.

The best way to begin to speak about a disorder is to describe its effect on a person. There may be a gradual or a sudden weakness of an arm or hand, a foot or a leg; a sensation of heaviness in the shoulders or a change in the nimbleness of the fingers. There may be a slight change in the vision of one or both eyes. There may be lightheadedness or dizziness.

Frequently, the condition lasts for just a short time, a few days or a few weeks perhaps, then it disappears. This is called a REMISSION. It is very difficult to know what to look for or where it might be. It is very awkward to suggest that a more complex problem may be underway when the simple statement of "It's the flu." or "It's a middle-ear infection." is more enthusiastically accepted.

As physicians administering treatment, we may be lulled into acquiescence when we give a medicine for a week and the severe balance disturbance from the inner ear resolves or, for that matter, any physical complaint. A lesion in the nervous system can be very small and will produce a small symptom, dependent on its position in the brain and then disappear in what we strangely call a remission. It may, some time in the future, return in a different way, in a different place. It could receive a different diagnosis, a different treatment, but again the remission. Eventually, in some people, the condition worsens and the horrible eventuality of paralysis results. Then the wheel chair, the bed and the final resting place follow. Some patients die within a few months. Others may live for thirty years. The final state of the bedridden, incontinent patient racked by painful flexor spasms of the lower limbs and shaken by febrile episodes of intercurrent infection is one of the most disturbing in medicine.

What is the cause? And at what stage do we diagnose it as an illness? The medical books give no hint of treatment. When the student in medical school reads the following statement, the condition can be dismissed as unimportant. . . .

"Despite the large number of remedies which may have been tried, no drug therapy appears to have any influence on the course of the disease. . .the most that can be done is to encourage and reassure the patient."

There is a tendency to overlook, to miss the incipient signs of Multiple Sclerosis until it is so far along that the patient volunteers his own diagnosis.

Let us look at the disease called MS with a sharp microscopic eye and seek clues that may suggest therapeutic approaches.

There are two obvious phenomena which occur simultaneously in a body associated with the production of Multiple Sclerosis and related diseases. One is a change in the nerve impulse pattern to the involved area. The other is the production of a type of clot within the capillary blood vessel supplying the nerve. Both ways show us therapeutic approaches. Let's analyze both of them.

There are two kinds of tissue within the brain and spinal cord. One has been referred to as the white matter. The white appearance comes from the fact that most of the nerve fibers in the white zone are myelinated. The white lipoid myelin sheath gives the white color. The other area is called the gray area. It is gray because it has non-myelinated fibers and a richer supply of blood.

It has frequently been demonstrated that the white substance of the nervous system is supplied or traversed by both trophic and autonomic (sympathetic and parasympathetic) fibers and cells. Therefore, it would be subjected to stimulatory responses from these fibers.

No matter what does it, the phenomenon that finally causes demyelination is inflammation. It happens this way:

DEMYELINIZATION

In Multiple Sclerosis, as well as other sclerotic conditions, an area of edema or swelling begins in connection with a nerve fiber. This occurs simultaneously with dilation of the blood vessels. The dilation and swelling are followed by a localized loss of myelin and the formation of fibrous scar tissue called gliosis.

It is difficult to tell whether dilation or demyelinization occurs first. But we know this. . . .the parasympathetic nervous system sends impulses to the brain tissues that cause the blood vessels to dilate. It also causes an increase in the permeability of the cells that make up the wall of the blood capillary. The result of an increase in permeability is the increased flow of fluid from the spaces around the blood vessel into the vessel causing it to fill. Simultaneous with this inflow of waste materials from the surrounding area, there is an increased movement of nutrients from within the blood vessel out into its environment to nourish the brain cells. If impulses from the trophic and parasympathetic systems are excessive or chronic, the permeability of the capillary wall will allow the movement of larger than desired molecules, such as fatty acids. A number of the fatty acids and aromatic organic acids have the capacity to dissolve myelin.

The myelin sheath appears to be necessary for proper nerve transmission. It is also capable of differential permeability so that it enters into the metabolism of the nerve fiber by controlling the movement of molecules through it. If it is destroyed, the nerve transmission falters and the nutrition to that segment of the nerve is altered.

Our interest naturally lies in the various phenomena that can produce damage to the myelin sheath. However, we must constantly bear in mind that demyelinization may not be the basis of Multiple Sclerosis, rather Multiple Sclerosis may be the cause of demyelinization. We must guard against the obvious pathology ending our search for the real culprit.

Here is a step-by-step description of the lesion that results in Multiple Sclerosis:

THE MULTIPLE SCLEROSIS LESION

1. Increased trophic or parasympathetic nerve impulse pattern transmission to the area.

2. Increased permeability with the dilation of blood

capillaries in the area.

3. Movement through the blood capillary wall of large molecules usually fatty acids or lipoproteins.

4. Foreign molecules enter the Schwann system and cause it to unravel.

5. Microglia migrating nerve cells come to the area and ingest the lipoid portions of the Schwann cell.

6. Round cells appear in the blood vessel and some proliferation occurs in the blood vessel wall.

7. The presence of microglia, endothelial cells and normal cells produce a scarring glial around the capillary.

8. This scarring organizes itself into a plaque, reducing the lumen of the vessel.

9. Blood flow through the vessel decreases and cells downstream become anoxic or oxygen starved.

10. The anoxia causes cellular damage which results in the release of histamine from the cells.

11. The histamine poisons adjacent cells, increasing their permeability.

12. The increased permeability permits movement of large molecular particles through the capillary wall.

13. With the continuation of item 3, a cyclic phenomenon begins.

14. Because of an increase in trophic or parasympathetic stimulation, the permeability of the adipose tissue fat cell is decreased, permitting the large chylomicron fats absorbed from the digestive tract to accumulate in the blood stream.

15. These large chylomicrons can enter into the openings of dilated blood vessel walls and leak into the surrounding tissues causing the inflammation, fibrosis and destruction of the Schwann cell.

PERMEABILITY

Several times now I have mentioned the word permeability. If we were to imagine the blood vessel wall, especially a very small one, as being a series of cells stuck together end to end by a cementing substance and if we were to imagine the cells and the cementing substances actually filled with tiny holes like a sieve, and if we were to imagine that particles in the blood stream leave it by passing through these little holes, we will be ready to understand permeability.

The size of the little holes determines the amount of seepage that will occur through them. The larger the holes, the more seepage. Now listen to this - The cementing substance between the cells consists of a mucopoly-saccharide called hyaluronic acid. If it is liquefied, the holes within it will get larger, hence its permeability increases. The enzyme that makes it dissolve is hyaluronidase. An increase of its activity results in a thinning of the hyaluronic. acid cementing substance, which makes the pores bigger which increases the permeability. The thing that increases the hyaluronidase activity is - are you ready for this - LEAD.

Wouldn't it be most reasonable to at least measure the lead level of the blood and remove whatever there is by adequate chelating techniques?

The next observations we should make are that heavy metals can be involved in the production of the problem. Their removal would, therefore, seem to be of major significance. We should also note that permeability is also affected by the nature of nerve transmissions going to the involved area. This opens the door to therapies capable of affecting nerve transmissions and permeability.

Now let us look at the degenerated area that actually is Multiple Sclerosis, the plaque.

The plaques are areas of swelling. Any blood vessels that might be flowing through the area are filled with basophils and microglia that are in turn filled with granular material or myelin debris. The vessels are dilated due to their increased permeability. Inflammation around cells arrive and a proliferation of cells occurs inside the blood vessel occluding its lumen.

Because of the increased trophic or cholinergic

stimulation, acetylcholine is released from the nerve endings. It increases the permeability of the endothelial cells lining the blood vessel. These cells release thromboplastin for the purpose of clot formation.

The fibrinogen level, therefore, should be measured and reduced if it is more than 25% higher than its minimum normal range. In this regard, an elevation of blood fibrinogen would be unwise. The acetylcholine also inhibits the anti-clotting chemical, heparin, which is brought to the area by the basophil cells. The basophil cells also liberate histamine. Histamine causes an increase in permeability of adjacent cells which results in more swelling, more clotting and more passage of protein molecules from the blood vessel into the tissue spaces. These foreign proteins then stimulate fibroblastic activity which begins the so-called hyaline degeneration.

SCLEROSIS

The basophil cells supply the raw materials and a hyaluronic acid type colloid substance is generated. The colloids chemically attract calcium, iron, phosphates, carbonates and magnesium. In other words, they get harder. The older and the harder they get, the more damage they do to blood vessels, lymph vessels and nerve fibers that go through them, thereby perpetuating the destructive phenomenon.

This observation tells us that extraction of the

precipitated minerals is a very important therapeutic approach.

The most important thing that can speed up this plaque phenomenon is increased permeability or fragility of the blood vessels, which in turn is caused by increased capillary pressure, trauma, anesthetics, toxins, heavy metals, acetylcholine, hyaluronidase and occlusion of lymphatic vessels.

I have mentioned that a very important enzyme present in the body can exert enormous influence on the status of the cementing substance in both nervous and blood vessel tissues. It is hyaluronidase. Hyaluronidase decreases the viscosity of hyaluronic acid. In other words, it destroys hyaluronic acid.

HYALURONIDASE

Here are some unusual facts about hyaluronidase:

1. Its presence in the body, in its activated form, elevates the blood uric acid level. This means that uric acid may indirectly be used as an indicator for hyaluronidase activity. An elevation of uric acid should alert us to more than just GOUT!

2. Ultra-violet radiation produces damage to hyaluronic acid similar to hyaluronidase. Prolonged exposure to sunlight should, therefore, be limited.

3. Hyaluronidase causes a resorption of protein in lymphatic vessels five to six times the normal amounts.

This osmotically pulls water out of the blood vascular system and, at the same time, produces obstruction of the lymph vessel if the condition persists too long. If an increased level of protein is permitted to exist for a long enough period, it will "coagulate" and not flow through the lymph vessels. The lymph vessels, if allowed to remain this way for a long time, will be permanently lost as a transport channel. This increases the permeability of adjacent lymph tissue and vascular capillary cells and the process becomes cyclic, perpetuating itself. This obstruction activates the mast cell release of histamine which starts another endless cycle of events leading to demyelinization and plaque formation.

4. Histamine opposes heparin.

5. Heparin opposes hyaluronidase.

6. Hyaluronidase increases acetylcholine action over that of adrenaline, which perpetuates the parasympathetic nerve dominance and here then we have a continuation of the trophic or cholinergic nerve impulse patterns that started the whole phenomenon in the first place.

7. Hyaluronidase produces a dilation of vessels and a vacuolation and breakdown of structure. It destroys cell bridges and removes intercellular cement substances, loosening up the epithelial and endothelial tissues.

8. Hyaluronidase enables phospholipase to diffuse more readily through tissues with even more necrosis or tissue destruction occurring.

9. Hyaluronidase prolongs muscle fatigue which is an undesirable feature in patients with Multiple Sclerosis.

As a matter of fact, cancers and tumors also produce hyaluronidase and by inactivating hyaluronic acid or heparin, it reduces the defenses of neighboring cells. This is one of the reasons that normal cells surrounding the cancer cell are destroyed. It is also one of the reasons that tumor cells can grow so independently. They use the destroyed cells for food.

ENVIRONMENTAL EFFECTS
ON MULTIPLE SCLEROSIS

Now let us observe some of the environmental features that can aggravate Multiple Sclerosis and, for that matter, any of the sclerotic neurologic diseases.

Exposure to cold is generally more beneficial to this kind of patient than is exposure to heat for several reasons. First, the marked increase in heat or body temperature, such as a fever, will cause a stimulation of the trophic or cholinergic nerves, increasing cellular permeability and aggravation of the condition. Second, the increase in heat causes a vasodilation of the peripheral blood vessels and reduces the amount of blood available for inner structures. This creates a degree of anoxia in the nervous system which aggravates the condition. Cold does the opposite and thereby is generally better tolerated. Extremes in either direction, however, should be avoided because of the resulting stress which further depletes an already crippled system.

EFFECT OF FATTY FOODS IN
MULTIPLE SCLEROSIS

The eating of more than minimal amounts of fatty foods provides an elevation of the chylomicron fats in the blood stream which aggravates the condition. The presence of increased blood fats produces a stickiness of the platelets and the red blood cells causing them to clump together in what is referred to as a rouleaux formation. These clumps could very easily plug up a very small capillary and begin or aggravate the conditions referred to earlier.

This observation leads us to specific dietary approaches as well as treatments which can unplug small blood and lymph vessels or unclump cellular components within the vessels, thereby allowing improved circulation. We can also see the application of therapies which can increase oxygen levels within cells, tissues and the blood stream.

The primary deprivation as a result of plugging of a capillary would be an oxygen deficiency. An oxygen deficiency results in the release of histamines by the starved cell and the process of degeneration begins. This "thickening" of the blood will naturally reduce the oxygen supplies to all tissues including, and especially, nerve tissues. Here, for example, is what fats in dairy products can do:

Following a large milk and cream meal, the available oxygen supply to the brain can be reduced by as much as 35%. Unsaturated oils, if taken in large amounts, can reduce available oxygen supplies by as much as 20%. Even skim milk can reduce the oxygen supply to the brain by 5%.

Let us now summarize everything that we have said in terms of possible therapeutic aids in the treatment of Multiple Sclerosis and related neurologic disorders.

TREATMENT OF MULTIPLE SCLEROSIS

The development of a sclerotic neurovascular disease is slow. It must be diagnosed early and treated early for best results. A thorough understanding of the symptoms that can appear early in a predominantly cholinergic nervous pattern is vital to detecting the disease potential and either preventing it or treating it. This nervous system imbalance can be treated in a number of ways: certain medicines like atropine, certain minerals like magnesium, certain vitamins like E and C, other nutrients like inositol and choline, stimulation of the adrenergic or depression of the cholinergic nervous systems by various modes of physical therapy like ultrasonics of specific ganglions and electrotherapy of the autonomic nervous system and the peripheral nervous system.

There should be an elimination of as much heavy metal poisoning as possible, metals such as lead, mercury, arsenic, cadmium and strontium. This can be done by the oral supplementation of specific chelated or amino acid complexed minerals such as magnesium, zinc, calcium and phosphorus and by specific amino acids such as methionine, glycine and cysteine. Activation of the glutathione detoxification enzyme system is very valuable. The most effective method of reducing blood borne heavy metals is with the use of short term intravenous infusions or long term oral preparations containing appropriate ion extracting agents.

There should be a maximum attempt to reduce the lipoprotein and chylomicron concentrations of the blood with the use of specific agents such as dietary controls with the elimination of fats, biologically assayed and standardized vitamin E, ascorbic acid, inositol, small amounts of thyroxine and certain amounts of bile salts to promote the flow of bile.

The metastatic accumulations of calcium in the plaques should be removed with intravenous ion extractor therapy specific for the removal of heavy metals and pathologically deposited calcium.

The myelin sheath should be supported by the use of specific nutrients such as glycine and serine amino acids, inositol and choline, the substrate vitamins necessary to promote the needed biochemical reactions such as pyridoxine, pantothenate, thiamine, B_{12} and niacinamide.

The prevention of lipid peroxidation or rancidity by vitamins E and C is very useful.

The reduction of the blood clotting factor, fibrinogen,

can be achieved nutritionally.

The use of agents that will inhibit hyaluronidase such as salicylate, heparin activator, magnesium, ascorbic acid, rutin, hesperidin, chelated copper and zinc are essential.

Obviously many of these things can be done for you only by your physician and a competent nutritionist, but here are some dietary suggestions that you can pursue yourself.

AVOID WHITE FLOUR

Avoid the use of all bleached flour products. Be aware of the fact that the words "whole wheat" are not an answer to this problem. Whole wheat products are frequently mixtures of bleached white flour and ground bran. An investigation of the bakeries you use and the flour mills from which they obtain their materials will clarify this dilemma.

AVOID HYDROGENATED FATS AND OILS

Avoid products containing hydrogenated or hardened oils. In the processing of hydrogenated fats, nickel compounds are used as catalysts. The most common nickel compounds used in this way are nickel carbonate hydroxide, nickel carbonyl and nickel formate. The industrial uses of nickel compounds is quite high and increased amounts enter our bodies constantly through air, water and the foods that we eat.

EFFECTS OF NICKEL

The principal pathologic action of nickel is enzyme inhibition by sulfhydryl group displacement and an increase in cellular permeability by incorporation with cellular potassium. This results in edema formation and hemorrhage, especially in the nervous system. The possibility of absorption of nickel from hydrogenated fats would thereby suggest that we eliminate these items from our diet. Crackers and baking mixes, frozen pies or prepared pie crusts, all margarines and many of the peanut butters should be avoided. French fries and potato chips prepared in oils or fats containing hydrogenated compounds should not be used. Fried foods should be avoided.

EFFECTS OF RANCIDITY

Any oil having the capacity of lipid peroxidation or rancidity should be eliminated, minimized or compensated for by adequate anti-oxidant supplementation. The free radicals that are developed by peroxidation conversions have the capacity to fracture amino acids thereby creating new chemical compounds in the body and also of rupturing the lysosome body in the cell which leads to cellular self-destruction. The practical avoidance of rancidity in the home would be as follows:

A marked reduction to zero, if possible, of coffee as a beverage. If it is used, it should be refrigerated and never reheated. Postum and Pero would be ideal substitutes.

Unsaturated oils should never be used in cooking. Olive or peanut oil is acceptable.

Butters are always preferable to margarines and sweet cream butter is preferred over ordinary butter.

Avoid tobacco because of lead, nicotine, coal tars, strontium, cadmium and insecticide contaminations. Avoid alcoholic beverages because of enzyme depletion, toxicity and the increase of permeability produced by alcohol, especially from the fusel oil it contains.

Avoid soft drinks, candy and pastries high in sugar.

FOOD RECOMMENDATIONS

The foods we have become accustomed to eating, as a result of childhood patterns, often are the most difficult habits we have to change. We are all a product of the type of likes and dislikes we developed early in life from the foods which were presented to us by our parents. In addition, most of us do not like to be told what not to eat. We usually moan, "There isn't anything left to eat." This diet is different. It tells you what you should eat. Try it, you'll find it is easy to follow and will bring about the changes necessary for your good health.

1. Do eat a bowl of oatmeal or other whole grain cereal every morning.

2. Do eat four cupfuls of vegetables daily - half raw and half cooked. It will surprise you how many vegetables really exist. Try them all.

3. Do eat one cupful of fruit daily, preferably raw, unless unavailable.

4. Do eat only the following fats: butter, olive oil, peanut oil. Margarine and unsaturated oils are the worst foods you can put into your body. (Flax seed oil, bottled in black and kept refrigerated, is the only exception - it can be used therapeutically at one tablespoonful once or twice daily.)

5. Do reduce coffee consumption to one cup or less daily. Get in the herb tea habit.

6. Do eat your heaviest meals at breakfast and lunch, light meal at night. This is the hardest rule to follow for most people.

7. Do eat a minimum of five servings of chicken, fish or turkey each week. You can have a serving of beef or pork occasionally. If you are a vegetarian by choice, eat seeds and nuts to supplement your diet. Eggs and dairy products may be used sparingly.

8. Do not combine fruits or fruit juices with

concentrated proteins (meats, dairy products, eggs), this will produce gas and discomfort.

9. Do eat whole grain, freshly baked breads and rolls.
10. Do use a seasoning salt made up of potassium, sodium, calcium, magnesium, lysine and kelp as your flavor enhancer.

11. Be positive and happy when you eat, your digestive system will work better. (We shouldn't have to tell you to avoid white sugar and white flour products as much as possible.)

Multiple Sclerosis - Abraham Hoffer, M.D.

Multiple Sclerosis has remained mysterious and very difficult to treat. In 1951, I directed a survey of all MS patients in Saskatchewan. About that time, surveys of prevalence had shown that MS was more common in cold countries like Canada. Thus, the prevalence in New Orleans was significantly lower than in Winnipeg. The Saskatchewan figures were about the same as for Manitoba, and recent surveys have shown they are still very bad.

The reasons for the effect of climate have not been discovered. Suggestions have been made that it is due to temperature or to the level of minerals in soil. The North American glaciers covered all of Canada and the northern United States, leaving behind soils rich in metals such as copper. Copper, although essential in trace amounts, is toxic and it was suggested these copper levels played a role. Perhaps other minerals were involved since copper toxicity does not cause MS-like symptoms.

The work of Horrobin (1977, 1979) and Rudin (1981) suggests that prostaglandins and their essential fatty acids precursors are involved. Evening primrose oil has been helpful to some patients with MS. Also, R. Swank found that diets low in fats derived from milk products were helpful. This indicates there is a fat involvement, but may also be due to allergic reactions to milk.

If temperature is a main factor, then one can develop a relationship. Animals and plants living in cold areas such as Canada, must have more unsaturated fatty acids to increase winter hardiness. That is why fish from cold waters, seals in northern Canada, and plant oils such as linseed oil and canola oil, are richer in omega-3 essential fatty acids (EFA) than animals in warm waters and warm plant oils such as olive, peanut and coconut oils. People living in Canada need more omega-3 EFA, but Rudin (1984) has shown that our modern diet contains only 20% of the EFA it contained 100 years ago. The change occurred when industry began to supply all our cooking oils, which are warm oils, low in EFA of the omega-3 type.

What would happen to a person predisposed to MS, living in a cold climate on a diet deficient of omega-3 EFA? Since winter hardiness is a function of the mass of the body, of which the brain is a minor component, then it is likely the limited quantities of EFA will be sequestered by the tissues most in need of winter hardiness properties, i.e., skin, subcutaneous tissues, muscles and ligaments. Any deficiency is apt to be shown in internal organs, including the central nervous system. Is this central deficiency of omega-3 essential fatty acids a key factor in allowing the MS changes in the nerves of the body? Is this a reason why MS is rarer in people living in warm areas, for there the overall need for EFA would be less and there would be less tendency for MS to occur? This hypothesis can be tested by studying dietary habits of patients with MS, compared to their relatives who are well and to people in warm areas. It can be tested further by restoring the balance between the two main groups of essential fatty acids and saturated fats. There is significant evidence that there are a number of MS syndromes, perhaps four or more. A few patients recover on an elimination diet, eliminating foods to which they are allergic or sensitive. A second group includes patients who have recovered on the F. Klenner (1973) multi-vitamin orthomolecular approach. A third group has recovered when treated effectively for chronic candidiasis. A fourth group may be mineral-sensitive. Until pure syndromes can be isolated, it may be impossible to run controlled, double-blind studies. Many patients can be helped, but many do not respond, perhaps because it is difficult to determine which group each patient falls into.

I am unhappy with the overall therapeutic response, especially from chronic patients with MS. When the illness is caught early, the results are much better. The patient must be very dedicated and powerfully motivated to follow the complicated treatments that have been used. They must contend with physicians who are opposed and discourage them, with the costs of treatment and with the slow pace of response. When every MS patient can be evaluated carefully using all the diagnostic measures and treated carefully with support from family and community agencies, the results will be much better than those achieved by palliative drug treatments alone.

ADDITIONAL INFORMATION

We include these references on MS because of the severity of the disease and the fact that what works in some cases does not necessarily work in others. This is research that deserves to be known, but we have not had the time to thoroughly check it out and declare it as valid from a clinical standpoint. You will note that we have given any author or group credit, plus as much information as possible so you may do your own research by going to a medical library. These are only abstracts, so you may wish the whole article.

Allergy & Histamine Treatment

This is a review article by *Dr. Hinton D. Jonez, M.D.* (May, 1952) on the treatment of Multiple Sclerosis (MS) utilizing allergy management, physical therapy and intravenous histamine. He notes it to be a prevalent condition. In review of autopsies of acute MS patients, he found that the changes that occurred in the nervous system were like infiltrates of fluid that greatly resembled localized allergic edema. The basis of his approach is that edema, or urticaria-like wheels, are scattered throughout the entire nervous system. The nervous system comes from the same embryologic layer (ectoderm) as the skin which has these reactions, but not in a hard, enclosed cavity. When allergic reactions occur in the bony cavity of the skull or spinal column, there is little room for expansion and there may be destruction of tissue due to increased pressure resulting in scarring or sclerotic plaque. If these urticaria wheels are reduced quickly enough, then symptoms will improve and further damage will not result. When the diagnosis of MS is made, supportive psychotherapy is warranted. Physical therapy is of great value in these patients. He utilized prostigmin, myanesin and curare as muscle relaxants, and as adjuncts to physical therapy. D-tubocurarine injections at 7.5 mg every fourth day up to 120 mg daily were utilized. It was merely a symptomatic treatment. They initially started with .25 cc daily, increasing or decreasing until the optimum dosage was achieved. He encouraged the avoidance of tobacco, chilling, accidents, over-exertion and emotional upsets. With the assumption that allergy is a cause of Multiple Sclerosis, histamine therapy was investigated. Histamine therapy was frequently utilized for life in his MS patients. The standard treatment regime was 2.75 mg of histamine diphosphate in 250 cc of normal saline, given at a rate of 30 to 60 drops/minute over 90 minutes for at least 30 treatments. Histamine therapy initially was five times a week for the first three weeks, then three times each week for the next five weeks. In serious cases, 11 mg of histamine diphosphate was given in a continuous infusion of 1,000 cc's of normal saline at a rate of 30 drops per minute every six hours, alternating with 11 mg of histamine diphosphate in 1,000 cc's of D5W. This infusion can be given for 24 to 48 hours as tolerated. At the time of this article, he had given over 60,000 intravenous infusions of histamine diphosphate without noticeable side effects. Reactions that did occur were suspected to be from a pyrogenic factor from improper sterilization or histamine being administered too rapidly. Failures may have occurred from too little histamine in too short a time. Strong vacoconstrictors such as tobacco must also be eliminated. Iontophoresis was a technique by which one could administer histamine through the skin using a galvanic current. It was perfect for home use and inexpensive. Sterile equipment was not needed. Subcutaneous injections did not seem to be as beneficial. A repository suspension was employed where histamine diphosphate 2.75 mg/cc in a menstruum of peanut oil and oxycholesterol derivatives was given by deep IM. The first dosage was usually .05 cc and then it was increased at a rate of .05 cc as tolerated until .5 cc was given daily. An extensive allergy approach was important in these patients and a detailed history and elimination of foods, molds, fungus, pollens and other miscellaneous allergens was employed. Most all MS patients have an allergy history. Elimination diets were utilized. He notes that Vitamin B-12, in large doses, had been given with reports of benefit. MS patients usually have hormonal deficiencies, especially of gonadotrophic hormones. The treatment outlined above does not cure MS, but it does arrest symptoms frequently. Bedridden patients become wheelchair bound, wheelchair patients become ambulatory and certain ambulatory patients become symptom-free. 9897

"Management of Multiple Sclerosis," Jonez, Hinton D., Postgraduate Medicine, May 1952;2:415-422 (Address: Postgraduate Medicine, McGraw Hill Healthcare Publications, 2 Prudential Plaza, 7th Floor, 108 N. Stetson Avenue, Chicago, IL 60601 USA)

Anti-Oxidant Therapy

Multiple Sclerosis in Scandinavian countries has been associated with low selenium levels. Anti-oxidant enzymes such as glutathione peroxidase and vitamins such as C and E have also been theorized to have benefit in Multiple Sclerosis. In this study, a single tablet containing vitamin C, 333 mg, vitamin E, 80 mg, and sodium selenite, 1 mg, was given at a dose of two tablets three times daily. In evaluating lymphocyte glutathione peroxidase (GSH-PX) of these 18 MS patients and 13 normal controls, it was found that the MS patients had almost 1/3 the GSH-PX levels. During the treatment, it found that GSH-PX values in the MS patients increased by a factor of three after three weeks and a factor of five after five weeks. Twenty MS patients receiving the above dosage or placebo were evaluated for side effects after two weeks and one month and no serious side effects were observed. In pharmacokinetic studies of ten

MS patients ingesting 1/3 of the above dose blood samples drawn at 0, 1, 3, 6, 12 and 24 hours had mean selenium levels rise from approximately 87-109 ug/l. This study confirms other studies that in MS patients GSH-PX activity is lower than in controls and that the GSH-PX levels in MS patients may be increased to supernormal levels without side effects. Sodium selenite is absorbed from these specially formulated tablets without hindrance from vitamin C. The authors conclude that a trial of high anti-oxidant supplementation in MS patients appears safe and acceptable. 6852

"High Dose Anti-oxidant Supplementation to MS Patients: Effects on Glutathione Peroxidase, Clinical Safety and Absorption of Selenium," Mai, Jesper, et al, <u>Biological Trace Element Research</u>, 1990;24:109-117. (Address: Jesper Mai, Department of Neurology, Arhus Kommunehospital, DK-8000 Arhus, Denmark)

Brain Magnesium

Four patients with Multiple Sclerosis were studied for brain magnesium concentrations and, compared to five controls utilizing coupled plasma emission spectrometery, it was found that the average magnesium content in the CNS tissue, as well as visceral organs, except the spleen, showed a significantly lower value in Multiple Sclerosis patients than controls. The most remarkable reduction of magnesium content was in the CNS white matter, including demyelinated plaques of MS samples. A chronic magnesium deficiency reduces the number of lymphocytes, especially T cells, resulting in derangements of the immune system. Magnesium and calcium ions are essential for the induction of lymphokine IL-2 that promotes division and proliferation of T cells. The lymphocyte in autoimmune disorders has a decreased ability to produce lymphokine IL-2 which may result from magnesium deficiency. Magnesium's metabolic role in the demyelinating process and Multiple Sclerosis needs further study. 8204

"Magnesium Concentration in Brains from Multiple Sclerosis Patients," Yasui, M., et al, ACTA Neurol. Scand., 1990;81:197-200. (Address: Masayuki Yasui, Division of Neurologic Diseases, Wakayama Medical Collage, 9 Bancho, Wakayama 640, Japan)

Colchicine (Oral)

Macrophages may be involved in the demyelination process in Multiple Sclerosis. Twenty-five patients with active Multiple Sclerosis took doses of oral colchicine up to 1.8 mg/d. Sixteen of those patients were stabilized or improved at ten months on the average. At 12 to 16 months, six patients were stable or improved. Side effects were predominantly gastrointestinal symptoms and could be managed by adjusting the dosage or symptomatic treatment. The authors conclude that colchicine has potential benefit as a prophylactic agent from the neurologic disability of MS with manageable side effects. 10227

"Preliminary Trial of Colchicine in Progressive Multiple Sclerosis," Annals of Neurology, July 1986;20(1):165-166. (Address: Herman J. Weinreb, M.D., Neurology, 530 1st Avenue, Suite 5A, New York, NY 10016, USA)

Colchicine (Intravenous)

Fifteen patients with active, chronic, progressive Multiple Sclerosis were given 1.5-3 mg weekly of intravenous colchicine. It was found that two patients had progression during the 14 months' average follow-up, but all patients continued the treatment. No patient became wheelchair bound. There were very minimal side effects, most notably soreness at the injection site. General stamina was noted to improve. Laboratory chemistries were not abnormal. The authors conclude that intravenous colchicine therapy should be investigated as a treatment for MS in blinded controlled trials. 10229

"Intravenous Colchicine in Chronic Progressive Multiple Sclerosis," Weinreb, Herman, M.D., Neurology, March 1989;39(Suppl. 1):318/PP462. (Address: Herman J. Weinreb, M.D., Neurology, 530 1st Avenue, Suite 5A, New York, NY 10016 USA)

Colchicine (Intravenous)

This correspondence reviews protocols for the use of intravenous colchicine in the treatment of MS. It is theorized that colchicine inhibits the inflammatory demyelinating activity of macrophages and, because of enhanced blood levels (ten fold higher than oral therapy), and the lack of side effects, is more advantageous than oral colchicine. The protocol includes intravenous colchicine at 1-3 mg weekly administered in a 6-10 cc syringe utilizing a 25-27 gauge butterfly needle (average patient 3 mg/wk). The major side effect is the possibility of extravasation, which can cause burning and aching of the limb or vein. It does not cause necrosis. Injectable colchicine comes in 1 mg/2ml ampules. It should be given over one to two minutes slow IV push. Alternating limbs weekly is important. If intense pain develops, the arm should be elevated for ten minutes and an ice pack should be used for at least 15 minutes. This can be repeated hourly. Delayed achiness or soreness of the arm can be treated with an injection of 1 cc of 1% lidocaine, which can be mixed with the colchicine solution. An alternative approach is mixing .25 cc of soluble betadexamethasone in the colchicine injection. Every three months a CBC, BUN, creatinine, SGOT, alkaline phosphatase, total bilirubin and CPK should be run. Sources for intravenous supplies are included. Protocols can be obtained upon request. 10230

"Clinical Protocol for the Use of Intravenous Colchicine in Multiple Sclerosis," Weinreb, Herman, M.D., Correspondence, September 25, 1990. (Address: Herman J. Weinreb, M.D., Neurology, 530 1st Avenue, Suite 5A, New York, NY 10016, USA)

Colchicine Therapy

This is a personal response on the effectiveness of oral colchicine versus intravenous colchicine in Multiple Sclerosis. The author states that 3 mgs given intravenously on a weekly basis is equivalent to approximately 30 mgs given orally per week. The daily dose then would be 4.28 mgs of colchicine by mouth. This would be a load that the gastrointestinal tract could probably not tolerate. For this reason, Dr. Weinreb used intravenous colchicine therapy on a weekly basis and rarely prescribes oral colchicine (he recommends the weekly intravenous colchicine at 1-3 mg/wk with 1 cc dexamethasone - see CP Currents August, 1991). 13602

"Colchicine Therapy in Multiple Sclerosis,": Personal Correspondence, July 30, 1991, pp. 1. (Address: Herman J. Weinreb, M.D., Neurology, New York University Medical Center, 530 1st Avenue, Suite 5A, New York, NY 10016, USA - 212-484-9045)

Protocols for Colchicine and Dexamethasone Therapy

"Multiple Sclerosis: Protocols for Colchicine and Dexamethasone Therapy," (this is a 7 page packet outlining the supplies, therapeutic protocol, side effects, laboratory assessment and general guidelines for colchicine therapy in Multiple Sclerosis), Weinreb, Herman J., M.D., Personal Correspondence, July 25, 1992;1-7. (Address: Herman J. Weinreb, M.D., Neurology, New York University Medical Center, 530 1st Avenue, Suite 5A, New York, NY 10016 USA - 212-484-9045) 13478

Low Saturated Fat Diet

This article reviews 144 Multiple Sclerosis (MS) patients on a low fat diet for 34 years. Patients who adhered to the low fat diet, which was less than 20 gm of fat daily, showed significantly less deterioration and much lower death rates than did those who consumed 20 gm or more of fat daily. The greatest benefit was seen in those with minimal disability at the start of the trial. There was less exacerbation of the illness in the low fat group. Deviating from the diet led to reactivation of the disease. More recently, patients on even more extreme fat restriction diets (10-15 gm/d) have had improvements in energy. Omitting red meat and dark meat poultry helps in lowering saturated fat. Supplements of essential unsaturated fatty acids up to 30 gm/d (2 oz of cod liver oil) have been reported to cause decreased relapse rates in MS. Increasing oil intake can decrease saturated fat intake as much as 2 gm for every 1 gm increase in oil intake. 9142

"Effect of Low Saturated Fat Diet in Early and Late Cases of Multiple Sclerosis," Swank, Roy Laver and Dugan, Barbara Brewer, The Lancet, July 7, 1990;336:37-39. (Address: Dr. R. L. Swank, Department of Neurology, Oregon Health Sciences University, Portland, OR 97201 USA)

Prostaglandin Production

Prostaglandin E2 (PGE2) and thromboxane B2 (TXB2) levels were evaluated in five chronic progressive Multiple Sclerosis (MS) patients as compared to two exacerbating or remitting MS patients and four healthy controls. It has been implicated that blood monocytes have been involved in the immune reactions which accompany demyelination in patients with Multiple Sclerosis. It was found that prostaglandin E2 released from the monocytes of the chronic MS patients was significantly higher than those obtained from the stable exacerbating or remitting MS patients and healthy controls. There was no difference in thromboxane B2 levels. It has been reported in the past that prostaglandin E2 peaks just prior to an exacerbation and then drops following MS exacerbations. These results are in agreement with these findings. Toxic oxygen metabolites, as well as prostaglandin E2, are increased in the monocytes of MS patients which suggests a continuing cycle of immune-mediated myelin destruction. The monocyte activation could occur from viruses or some dysfunctioning of cell mediated immunity. Peripheral monocytes do cross the blood brain barrier and can be found at sites of demyelination. Arachidonic acid metabolism may also be involved. 9583

"Prostaglandin Production in Chronic Progressive Multiple Sclerosis," Aberg, Judith A., et al, The Journal of Clinical Laboratory Analysis, 1990;4:246-250. (Address: Laurence M. Demers, M.D., Professor of Medicine and Pathology, Penn State College of Medicine, P.O. Box 850, Hershey, PA 17033 USA)

Vascular-Ischemic Model and Hyperbaric Oxygen

This hypothesis suggests that Multiple Sclerosis is a cerebrovascular-ischemic disease resulting from a "wound" in the central nervous system initiated by a local hypertension with subsequent vascular injury, edema and ischemic hypoxia. These effects cause demyelination, the initial insult to the nervous system, followed by a secondary effect from the immune system. The author reviews the role of thromboxanes (A2), edema, the immune response and reactive oxygen species. The author notes that the immune system is abnormal in MS but states it is not known whether this abnormality is a cause or an effect. He states there is no direct evidence that MS has an immunologic etiology, is caused by a virus, or is of autoimmune origin. He suggests that hyperbaric oxygen therapy is an important modality for early and chronic MS to stimulate "wound" healing of the CNS utilizing the Neubaurer low pressure protocol (at the onset, no greater than 1.5 ATA, increasing gradually over days or weeks). Hyperbaric oxygen therapy treats the hypoxia associated with inflammation, edema and ischemia. Hyperbaric oxygen therapy in other conditions has been used to reduce edema in decompression sickness, intracranial pressure from head and spinal cord injuries, and controls the edema in trauma and non-trauma situations. It can reduce pressure in compartment syndrome and has benefits in wound healing, skin grafts and burns. It also has anti-inflammatory properties. 10754

"The Etiology of Multiple Sclerosis: A New and Extended Vascular-Ischemic Model," Gottlieb, S.F., et al, Medical Hypothesis, 1990;33:23-29. (Address: S.F. Gottlieb, Department of Biological Sciences, University of South Alabama,

Vitamin B-12 and Macrocytosis

Twenty-seven patients with Multiple Sclerosis had mild but significant macrocytosis when compared to neurologic controls. The authors conclude their observations of mild macrocytosis, in conjunction with other studies that have shown decreased CSF vitamin B12 levels in MS patients, should encourage further study of vitamin B12 metabolism in this disorder. 8839

"Multiple Sclerosis and Macrocytosis," Crellin, R.F., et al, ACTA Neurol Scand., 1990;81:388-391. (Address: E. H. Reynolds, Department of Neurology, Kings College Hospital, Denmark Hill, London SE5 9RS England)

Vitamin B12 Deficiency

This is a case study of a 46 year old female with painful paresthesias associated with right leg weakness with a presumptive diagnosis of Multiple Sclerosis. For 15 years, this patient was admitted approximately every 18 months for exacerbation of symptoms and treated with ACTH infusions with improvement. In June of 1987, magnetic resonance imaging showed abnormalities in the white matter and two months later, an MCV was done and it was elevated at 100.8. She was seen by this group five months later at age 61 and had developed severe spastic monoparesis of the right leg with wasting. She had abnormal vibration appreciation in the feet and pin prick appreciation in the mid-thigh on the right. MCV at that time was 98.3 and serum vitamin B12 level as 100 pg/ml and folic acid was 8.2 mg/ml. Serum intrinsic factor anti-bodies were present. Serum homocysteine and methylmalonic acid levels were normal. The patient received vitamin B12 injections of 1,000 ug daily for one week, followed by weekly injections. Six months after receiving vitamin B12, she had increased right leg strength and her MCV had gone down to 92.7 and her B12 had elevated to just within normal range and homocysteine and methylmalonic acid levels were reduced. They believe that this neurologic syndrome was caused by vitamin B12 deficiency and this possibly suggests a link between vitamin B12 and Multiple Sclerosis. They conclude that all patients diagnosed as having Multiple Sclerosis should be screened for possible underlying B12 deficiency, especially since patients with vitamin B12 deficiency may present with neurologic complications in the absence of anemia and hematologic abnormalities. 8624

"Vitamin B12 Deficiency and Multiple Sclerosis," Ransohoff, Richard M., The Lancet, May 26, 1990;1285-1286. (Address: Richard M. Ransohoff, Department of Neurology, Molecular Biology, Brain and Vascular Research and Laboratory of Hematology, Cleveland Clinic Foundation, Cleveland, OH 44195-5139 USA)

Vitamin B12 Deficiency

This study evaluated 10 patients for the association of Multiple Sclerosis and unusual vitamin B12 deficiency. Presentations of the cases were typically classic for Multiple Sclerosis. Eight cases began before the age of 40, which is a rare age range for vitamin B12 deficiency. Nine patients had hematologic abnormalities, but only 2 were anemic. Six of the ten patients had low erythrocyte cobalamin levels. Only 2 of 10 patients had pernicious anemia. There was no explanation for the remaining B12 deficiencies. It is thought that there was a problem with vitamin B12 binding and/or transport. The authors feel that, in these particular cases, the association between vitamin B12 deficiency and Multiple Sclerosis was more than coincidence. The authors note that empiric B12 injections have been used for over 30 years in the treatment of Multiple Sclerosis. Originally, patients have noted marked improvement and neurologic benefit. Several studies are reviewed of serum and cerebrospinal spinal fluid B12 levels in Multiple Sclerosis during 1956 and 1965. These studies were done because of the demyelination aspect seen in Multiple Sclerosis and vitamin B12's role in myelination. In the 60's, large studies found negative or equivocal results for the relationship between low serum and cerebrospinal fluid B12 levels and Multiple Sclerosis. Subsequently, much of the interest in vitamin B12 studies "died." The authors state that the findings in these 10 patients should reawaken the interest in the role of B12 in Multiple Sclerosis. The authors note a retrospective survey of admissions to a neurology ward at King's College Hospital in London, England over a 1 year period which showed that Multiple Sclerosis patients had mild but significant macrocytosis compared to an age matched control group. This was first reported over 30 years ago and has been overlooked. These authors have confirmed significant macrocytosis in MS patients, and have also found in them a decrease of serum vitamin B12 levels and elevation of plasma unsaturated R-binder levels. Lower cerebrospinal fluid levels have recently been reported in Multiple Sclerosis. There appears to be some similar HLA antigen associations between Multiple Sclerosis and pernicious anemia. 13557

"Multiple Sclerosis Associated with Vitamin B12 Deficiency," Reynolds, E.H., et al, <u>Archives of Neurology</u>, August 1991;48:808-811. (Address: E.H. Reynolds, M.D., Department of Neurology, King's College Hospital, Denmark Hill, London SE5 9RS England)

<u>Vitamin B12 Metabolism, Macrocytosis and Homocysteine</u>

This is a review article on the possibility that vitamin B12 deficiency may be associated with Multiple Sclerosis (MS). It is noted that Multiple Sclerosis is usually clinically and pathologically clearly distinguishable from vitamin B12 deficiency, although both have in common the demyelination of the nervous system. Older research has shown slightly larger than normal red blood cells (macrocytosis) in Multiple Sclerosis patients. One study has shown significant lowering of serum vitamin B12 and elevation of plasma unsaturated R-binder capacity. The function of R-binder is unknown, but there are 3 case reports in the literature of a possible association of MS with R-binder deficiency. Another researcher, using a sophisticated assessment technique, has reported significantly lower CSF vitamin B12 in MS patients. Serum levels of vitamin B12, which have been the means of assessing B12 status in the past, are not a reliable guide to tissue vitamin B12 deficiency. Recently, it has been shown that homocysteine may play an important role in diagnosing functional vitamin B12 deficiency. In this author's study, they found that plasma homocysteine levels were significantly elevated and negatively correlated with serum vitamin B12, suggesting that low levels of vitamin B12 in MS are associated with a functional deficiency, even in the absence of overt hematologic alterations. Two possible explanations of the association between MS and vitamin B12 are that:

1. The vitamin B12 deficiency, regardless of its cause, renders some patients more vulnerable to putative viral-immunological mechanisms widely suspected in MS.

2. The chronic immune reaction, or recurrent myelin repair process, increases the need for vitamin B12.

In evaluating the hypothesis of vitamin B12 deficiency playing a role in MS, the following needs to be considered:

1. In the clinical setting, the distinction between Multiple Sclerosis and "subacute combined degeneration" due to vitamin B12 deficiency can lead to difficulty in the diagnosis.

2. There are some case reports in the literature in which a diagnosis of Multiple Sclerosis has been suspected, only to be changed following the discovery of abnormal vitamin B12 metabolism.

3. None of the patients with MS and unequivocal vitamin B12 deficiency have the typically expected neurologic manifestation of this deficiency state.

4. Demyelinization in the spinal cord and brain, are important features of vitamin B12 deficiency and inborn

errors of metabolism.

5. Recently, a myelopathy, which neuropathologically resembles a subacute combined degeneration, has been seen in AID's patients in the absence of vitamin B12 deficiency. It is not clear whether the mechanisms are viral or metabolic.

The author feels that, at the very least, one should ask the question of whether the association of vitamin B12 deficiency from any cause is aggravating the underlying Multiple Sclerosis or the process of remyelination. He notes that for years vitamin B12 injections have been given predominantly as a placebo in the treatment of Multiple Sclerosis. Some patients subjectively state they feel better with this therapy, even though no controlled trial to support this conviction is available. The author encourages more research to be done on the role of vitamin B12 in the treatment of neuropathological disorders. 16150

"Multiple Sclerosis and Vitamin B12 Metabolism," Reynolds, E.H., Journal of Neurology, Neurosurgery and Psychiatry, 1992;55:339-340. (Address: E.H. Reynolds, Department of Neurology, Maudsley and King's Collage Hospitals, Denmark Hill, London)

Zinc and Environmental Factors
Multiple Sclerosis, like other autoimmune disease, may have a genetic predisposition expressed in HLA antigens. A large number of environmental toxins such as the heavy metal cadmium, pesticides, and solvents have neurotoxic effects. Marginal zinc deficiency occurs frequently in our society. In cases of genetic

predisposition, combined with environmental factor (i.e. cold and neurotoxic agents) marginal zinc deficiency prolonged by stress may allow Multiple Sclerosis to develop. Prevention of Multiple Sclerosis may occur by early HLA typing and modifying risk factors such as environmental toxin exposure and zinc deficiency early on in life. 6017

"The Role of Environmental Factors and Pollutants in Combination with Genetic Predisposition in the Etiology of Multiple Sclerosis: Possibilities for Prevention?" Morselt, A.F.W., Ph.D., Journal of Child Neurology, July 1989;4:228-229. (Address: A.F. Morselt, Ph.D., Laboratory of Histology and Cell Biology, University of Amsterdam, Academic Medical Center, Meibergdreef 15, 1105 AZ, Amsterdam, The Netherlands)

Cigarette Smoking and Motor Function

This study evaluated the effect of cigarette smoking on motor function in 21 patients with Multiple Sclerosis and 11 healthy controls. Sixteen of 21 patients had a transient deterioration of their motor function immediately after smoking, lasting for 10 minutes. The mean decrease in motor function score for all 21 patients was 14%. When the same motor function tests were done without smoking, only 3 of 14 patients had a deterioration and the group had a mean improvement of 8%. The control group showed a steady improvement over time, both in smoking and in simulation experiments. The authors conclude that cigarette smoking can cause a transient deterioration in motor functioning in certain patients with Multiple Sclerosis, probably due to the central nervous system effects of nicotine. 17481

"Effects of Cigarette Smoking on Motor Functions in Patients with Multiple Sclerosis," Emre, Murat, M.D. and De Decker, Katherine, Archives of

Neurology, December 1992;49:1243-1247. (Address: Murat Emre, M.D., Clinical Research, CNS Department, Sandoz Pharma Ltd., 4002, Basel, Switzerland)

Interferons

Multiple Sclerosis (MS) is an inflammatory demyelinating disease in which current treatment is generally symptomatic; corticotrophin or corticosteroids for acute exacerbations or more potent immunosuppressive drugs, in cases that do not respond to steroids. Interferons have been an area of increasing interest in Multiple Sclerosis, with recent evidence suggesting that interferons may effect MS by mediating immunoregulatory, rather than anti-viral or non-specific mechanisms. It is noted that interferon ɣ increases the exacerbation rate while interferon ß (Bioferon) tends to inhibit the activity of interferon ɣ and appears to prevent disease activity. Recently, interferon ß was given in a large multi-center, placebo-controlled trial with positive enough results at 2 years of treatment, that a license for its clinical use was submitted to the FDA in June of 1992. This study will continue, double-blind, for at least another year, and a second trial of systemic, recombinant interferon ß therapy is also in progress. In the multi-center trial, which was double-blind and placebo controlled, over 350 subjects with clinically definitely relapsing MS were enrolled. The subjects were randomized to receive either high dose, 45 million units, or low dose, 9 million units, of interferon ß-SER-17 or a placebo by subcutaneous injection every other day for 2 years. In the next study which has gotten underway, interferon ß will be given at 6 million units of interferon, or a placebo, and administered weekly by intramuscular injection for 2 years in these relapsing Multiple Sclerosis patients. 17520

"Interferons and Multiple Sclerosis: A Review of the Evidence," Panitch, Hillel S., Drugs, 1992;44(6):946-962. (Address: Dr. Hillel S. Panitch, Department of Neurology, University of Maryland School of Medicine, 22 South Green Street, Baltimore, MD 21201 USA)

Intravenous Immune Globulin

This study evaluated 10 patients with relapsing-remitting Multiple Sclerosis who were given intravenous immune globulin at .4g/kg/d for 5 consecutive days, and then a booster dose of immune globulin at .4 g/kg every 2 months for the next 12 months, and compared them to 10 untreated patients with a similar type of Multiple Sclerosis. The exacerbation rate was reduced from 3.7 per year before treatment to 1.0 per year during treatment in immune-globulin treated patients, while the frequency of exacerbations remained unaltered in the control subjects. The post treatment Kurtzke Expanded Disability Status Scale score was reduced from a mean of 4.45 to 4.15, whereas in controls, it increased from 3.5 to 3.75. These results suggest that immune globulin can reduce the ongoing pathologic process in Multiple Sclerosis, and appears to be a promising treatment in the prevention of exacerbations. The immune globulin (Gaminume N) was obtained from Miles Inc., Cutter Biological in Promedico, Israel. The substance was given in a sterile 4.5% to 5.5% solution of human protein in 9% to 11% maltose. 17482

"Open Controlled Therapeutic Trial of Intravenous Immune Globulin in Relapsing-Remitting Multiple Sclerosis," Achiron, Anat, M.D., Ph.D., et al, <u>Archives of Neurology</u>, December 1992;49:1233-1236. (Address: Anat Achiron, M.D., Department of Neurology, Beilinson Medical Center, Petah-Tiqva, 49100 Israel)

MUSCULAR
DYSTROPHY

MUSCULAR DYSTROPHY

There are several types of Muscular Dystrophy, as evidenced by the chart on the next page. It is thought that it is an inherited disease and the probability of transmission through the family tree is explained in the chart on page 75. The cause is even more vague than the origin of Muscular Dystrophy and the slow progressive degeneration of the muscle fibers is very frustrating because so little therapy is available.

All is not lost, however, when we consider the wholistic philosophy of health. First of all, the body is a dynamic and constantly changing organism. Nothing is broken, never to be fixed - the body constantly wants to repair itself. In Muscular Dystrophy, there is a serious neuromuscular problem that must be addressed.

Considering that it is a well known fact that the muscles receive all their direction from the nerves and, in this disease, the muscles seem to be without the stimulation of movement necessary for growth and maintenance of tone, we really must look at the nerves as a possible source of the problem.

The use of very special wave forms of low current electrical stimulation has been quite beneficial to many individuals with Muscular Dystrophy. Unfortunately, there are very few of these special wave form generators at this time. There were only a very limited number made many years ago in an army rehabilitation center after World War II where they were used to benefit soldiers who had suffered battlefield wounds which involved their nervous systems. We are fortunate in having such a unit at Hospital Santa Monica and guard it with great care.

TYPES OF MUSCULAR DYSTROPHY

Duchenne Muscular Dystrophy

In this type, the child is slow in learning to sit up and walk, and does so much later than normal. The condition is rarely diagnosed before the age of 3, but progresses rapidly. Affected children tend to walk with a waddle and have difficulty climbing stairs. In getting up from the floor, the child "climbs up his legs," pushing his hands against his ankles, knees and thighs. Sometimes there is curvature of the spine. Despite their weakness, the muscles (especially those in the calves) appear bulky; this is because wasted muscle is replaced by fat. By about age 12, affected children are no longer able to walk; few survive their teen years, usually dying from a chest infection or heart failure. Affected boys often have below-average intelligence.

Becker's Muscular Dystrophy

This type produces the same symptoms as the Duchenne type, but starts later in childhood and progresses much more slowly. Patients often reach the age of 50. Both types of dystrophy have sex-linked inheritance.

Myotonic Dystrophy

This form affects muscles of the hands and feet. Infants are floppy and slow to develop. The main feature is that the muscles contract strongly but do not relax easily. Myotonic Dystrophy is associated with cataracts in middle age, baldness, mental retardation, and endocrine problems. The condition has an autosomal dominant pattern of inheritance.

Limb-Girdle Muscular Dystrophy

This type takes different forms. It starts in late childhood or early adult life, and progression is slow. The muscles of the hips and shoulder are mainly affected. Other nerve and muscle conditions must be eliminated before this form of dystrophy can be diagnosed confidently.

Facioscapulohumeral Muscular Dystrophy

This form usually appears first between the ages of 10 and 40; it affects only the muscles of the upper arms, shoulder girdle and face. It is inherited in an autosomal dominant pattern. In this form of Muscular Dystrophy, progression of the weakness is slow and severe disablement is rare.

Nutritional Aspects

The use of phosphatidyl choline (the nutritionally effective ingredient in lecithin) as a supplement in the amount of 10 grams daily has shown some improvement in as little as 15 days.

Vitamin E and selenium, powerful anti-oxidants, have been used in the amounts of vitamin E (d-alpha tocopherol) 2,000 IU and 3 mg of sodium selenite, showed partial regression of all symptoms including muscular weakness, myopathic facies, bilateral ptosis and mental tiredness. This study was repeated with similar results in a European country. It is well worth following for several months since the benefits did not occur until 6 months or more into the treatment.

Vitamin E alone was also successful, but only partially so in many studies. It is interesting that a condition in cows, very similar to Muscular Dystrophy, responds beautifully to oral supplementation of vitamin E, but the same is not true for the human race. So remember your selenium!

A more recent publication from India discusses using vitamin E with inositol and getting very promising results in Muscular Dystrophy. Maybe the best nutritional supplement program would look like this:

Vitamin E	2,000 IU
Inositol	2,000 mg
Sodium Selenite	3 mg

The following abstracts of recent articles are considered to be of interest to anyone with this disease. You can contact your local medical library for complete copies of any of these abstracts.

MUSCULAR DYSTROPHY

Vitamins and Trace Elements

Twenty-four patients with Muscular Dystrophy were evaluated for vitamin and trace element status. Special areas of interest were vitamin E and selenium since they have been reported in other areas to be involved with protection against lipid peroxidation and also may have some benefit in this disorder. In this study, no deficiency was seen in trace elements or vitamins but, there were low blood levels of selenium found in some children, justifying supplementation. There were also very low levels of vitamin D, which is associated with disorders of phosphorous metabolism. The authors conclude that calcium/phosphorous metabolism and vitamin D status needs to be evaluated and normalized to optimize bone growth. 6758

"Vitamin and Trace Element Status in Children with Progressive Muscular Dystrophy," Voirin, J., et al, Trace Elements in Medicine, 1989;6(4):165-168. (Address: Dr. J. Voirin, Neuromuscular Pathology Consultation, CHRU Clemenceau, Caen Cedex, France)

Vitamin E in Ruminants

It is know that selenium and vitamin E deficiency in ruminants causes a nutritional Muscular Dystrophy. This dystrophy affects the muscle system and myocardium and can present in acute and chronic forms. Stress has been known to induce a subclinical myopathy in adult animals. Diagnosing this nutritional Muscular Dystrophy should be based on a physical examination and biochemical studies, which includes muscle enzyme activities in the blood and serum selenium and vitamin E concentrations. The treatment should attempt to correct the vitamin E and selenium deficiency. 15972

"Nutritional Muscular Dystrophy from Deficiencies of Selenium and Vitamin E in Ruminants," Garcia-Belenguer, S., et al, Med. Vet., 1992;9(2):84-92. (Address: S. Garcia-Belenguer, Department De Patologia Animal De La Facultad De Veterinaria De La Universidad De Zaragoza, Miguel Servet 177, 50013-Zaragoza)

Free Radicals

Oxidative stress resulting in tissue damage has been hypothesized as the cause of many of the structural, functional and biochemical alterations that occur in inherited Muscular Dystrophy in humans and animals. There is indirect evidence in Muscular Dystrophy of an accumulation of byproducts from oxidative damage that results in a compensatory increase in cellular anti-oxidants, alterations in proportions and metabolism of cellular lipids, abnormal functioning of cellular membranes, altered activities of membrane-bound enzymes, and disturbances in cellular protein turnover and energy production. Manipulation of free radical fluxes in tissues by nutritional manipulation or other means, can induce muscle injury which mimics the biochemistry and pathology of Muscular Dystrophy. Several theories are discussed as the cause of Duchenne Muscular Dystrophy. Included are the neurogenic theory, vascular ischemia and hormonal theory, developmental block theory, the role of the immune system, proteolysis and the free radical theory. The free radical theory of oxidative injury to muscle cells is a hypothesis which can explain most, if not all, the structural function or biochemical changes that are characteristic or many neuromuscular disorders, including Muscular Dystrophy. The measurement of dystrophic muscle fibers has shown an increased content of byproducts of oxidative damage, a compensatory increase in cellular anti-oxidants, changes in proportions and metabolism of cellular lipids, abnormal functioning of cellular membranes, altered activities of membrane bound enzymes such as Ca^{2+}ATPase, alterations in cellular protein turnover and energy production. Research has shown that endogenous anti-oxidants and anti-oxidant enzymes are present at elevated levels in muscles from Duchenne Muscular Dystrophy patients. This is the normal compensatory mechanism for oxidative stress. Vitamin E is critical to normal muscle function. The theory that a defect in vitamin E metabolism is the underlying cause of Muscular Dystrophy was first formulated 41 years ago, but has generally been rejected. The authors note that early investigations had relatively insensitive techniques for assessing vitamin E levels in the muscle. Even with the indirect evidence mentioned previously, there is still no firm evidence of vitamin E's benefit in this disorder. The author feels that, based on studies published over the last 40 years, free radical induced injury appears unlikely to play a primary role in the tissue injury associated with Muscular Dystrophy. Exogenous anti-oxidants are not deficient in the dystrophic muscle, and enhanced production of radicals by dystrophic tissues has not been measured. Therapeutic use of anti-oxidants has not resulted in a significant benefit in dystrophic humans or animals. The absence of dystrophin is the critical defect in Duchenne and Becker's Muscular Dystrophy. The function and pathological role of this protein in different forms of this disease is unknown. The membrane location of dystrophin suggests that the absence of this protein may predispose these structures to oxidative injury. Despite changes indicative of free radical injury in dystrophic muscle, current evidence does not support the hypothesis that free radicals play a causative role in muscle damage. It does remain possible though that this mechanism is involved in secondary tissue injury associated with some forms of Muscular Dystrophy. The author closes by saying that the inconclusive role for oxidative stress in Muscular Dystrophy, despite the extensive research, re-emphasizes the problems encountered when trying to establish free radicals as a significant factor in human diseases. 17599

"Free Radicals and Muscular Dystrophy," Kehrer, James P. and Murphy, Michael E., Free Radical Mechanisms of Tissue Injury, CRC Press, 1992:chapter 10;190-200. (Address: James P. Kehrer/Michael E. Murphy, College of Pharmacy, University of Texas, Austin, TX 68712-1074 USA)

A L S

(Amyotrophic Lateral Sclerosis)
(Lou Gehrig's Disease)

Amyotrophic Lateral Sclerosis
(Lou Gehrig's Disease)

I always considered it a shame that Lou Gehrig, a truly great baseball player, will be remembered for having a disease named after him rather than his feats in the ballpark. Amyotrophic Lateral Sclerosis is another disease of the nervous system affecting the motor neurons.

The onset of ALS is usually after the age of 40 and it affects more males that it does females. Muscular weakness and atrophy usually begins in the hands and spreads to the forearms and legs. Often the swallowing reflex is lost, making it necessary to tube feed the patient. Few patients live beyond five years after diagnosis and those that do are usually totally incapacitated.

Unfortunately, wholistic therapy is very weak in this disease, although some scattered research is bringing some hope. We have printed them here for your review.

Glutamate, Amino Acids
Amyotrophic Lateral Sclerotic patients have defective glutamate metabolism with varying levels of excitatory amino acids in the central nervous system. A current hypothesis is that altered presynaptic glutamatergic mechanisms may cause neuroexcitotoxic cell loss. High local concentrations of glycine may cause abnormal

potentiation of excitatory transmissions mediated by glutamate receptors and subsequent loss of motoneurons. In a previous double-blind study using branch chain amino acids in 22 patients, the author reports that after one year, the branch chain amino supplementations showed significant benefit in maintaining strength in extremity muscles and the ability to ambulate. Further studies are warranted. 9280

"Glutamate Dysfunction and Selective Motoneuron Degeneration in Amyotrophic Lateral Sclerosis: A Hypothesis," Plaitakis, Andreas, M.D., Annals of Neurology, July 1990;28(1):3-7. (Address: Andreas Plaitakis, M.D. Mt. Sinai School of Medicine, 1 Gustave Levy Place, New York, NY 10029 USA)

Trace Elements in Hair
(Manganese, Mercury, Selenium)

Hair trace elements were assessed in 11 cases of Amyotrophic Lateral Sclerosis (ALS), over 1,400 healthy individuals, and 11 cases of cerebrovascular disease. The only abnormalities found were elevated hair manganese concentrations in the ALS patients as a whole. One ALS patient had elevated hair mercury while two other ALS patients had elevated hair selenium concentrations. The authors encourage further study of trace elements' role in the pathogenesis of ALS. 11348

"Hair Trace Elements in Amyotrophic Lateral Sclerosis," Oishi, M., et al, Trace Elements in Medicine, 1990;7(4):182-185. (Address: Dr. M. Oishi, Department of Neurology, Nihon University School of Medicine, 30-1 Oyaguchi-Kamimachi, Itabashi-Ku, Tokyo 173, Japan)

Aluminum in the Central Nervous System

This is a case report of 2 patients with Amyotrophic Lateral Sclerosis who, upon metal analysis, were found to have significantly higher aluminum concentrations in their central nervous systems. They also had higher calcium and calcium/magnesium ratios and lower magnesium concentrations when compared to controls. Neither of these patients was exposed to toxic environmental factors or had a past history of neurologic disease. Upon postmortem, there was found motor neuronal death and degeneration of the pyramidal tracks. Low calcium, magnesium and high aluminum levels in the soil and drinking water have been suggested as partially responsible environmental factors in the pathogenesis of Amyotrophic Lateral Sclerosis. Other studies have shown abnormalities in calcium, magnesium and aluminum metabolism in the pathogenesis of ALS. Calcium metabolism dysfunction appears to be important in ALS. In animal models, rabbits fed low calcium/magnesium diets, with oral supplementation of aluminum, developed spheroids in the anterior horn cells of the spinal cord and accumulation of neurofilmaments in the anterior horn. In a monkey model of animals on low calcium/high aluminum diets, mild calcium and aluminum deposition and degenerative changes in the motor neurons of the spinal cord, brain stem, substantia nigra and the cerebrum have been observed. These two particular patients had no exposure to higher aluminum in the environment. It is suggested that abnormal

84

metabolism of calcium and magnesium, in addition to aluminum exposure, may have caused motor neuron death and degeneration of the pyramidal tracts in these patients. Further study is needed on the hypothesis of high aluminum deposition in the central nervous system and its role in the pathogenesis of ALS. 12987

"High Aluminum Deposition in Central Nervous System of Patients with Amyotrophic Lateral Sclerosis From The Kii Peninsula, Japan: Two Case Report," Yasui, M., et al, <u>Neurotoxicology</u>, 1991;12:277-284. (Address: Dr. Masayuki Yasui, Division of Neurologic Diseases, Yakayama Medical Collage, 9 Bancho, Wakayama 640, Japan)

Calcium, Magnesium and Aluminum Metabolism

The association of Amyotrophic Lateral Sclerosis in the Western Pacific with low calcium and magnesium and high aluminum concentrations was evaluated in an animal model. Rats were given either a standard diet with low calcium, low calcium and magnesium or low calcium and magnesium with high aluminum for 90 days. In another separate study, Japanese macaques were fed diets normal in calcium, low in calcium, low in magnesium, low in calcium and magnesium or low in calcium and magnesium with added aluminum for 4 weeks. It was found that calcium and magnesium levels in the lumbar vertebra and femur were significantly reduced, and bone aluminum levels significantly increased in rats fed diets deficient in calcium alone or diets low in calcium and magnesium with or without aluminum. Aluminum content was also higher in rats fed the calcium deficient diet. In monkeys fed the low calcium/magnesium diet with added aluminum, there was found reduced serum levels of calcium, magnesium, serum parathyroid hormone, bone, GLA-protein and alkaline phosphatase. The authors conclude that the data suggests that altered bone metabolism from chronic dietary deficiency of calcium increased the mobilization of calcium and magnesium from bone and calcium deposition in the brain. Aluminum is known to accumulate in the mitochondria of osteoblasts and in the lysosomes of the central nervous system tissue. Aluminum deposition in the central nervous system may result in neurofibrillary degeneration. 13919

"Evaluation of Magnesium, Calcium and Aluminum Metabolism in Rats and Monkeys Maintained on Calcium-Deficient Diets," Yasui, Masayuki, et al, Neurotoxicology, 1991;12:603-614. (Address: Dr. Masayuki, Yasui, Division of Neurological Diseases, Wakayama Medical College, 9 Bancho, Wakayama 640, Japan)

EMBRACING WHOLISTIC HEALTH

by Kurt W. Donsbach, D.C., N.D., Ph.D.

CLARIFYING THE
BODY-MIND-SPIRIT
CONNECTION
in
CANCER * ARTHRITIS * CANDIDIASIS
HEART DISEASE * MULTIPLE SCLEROSIS

Explicit treatment protocols from the world famous natural healing insitutions - Hospital Santa Monica, Hospital St. Augustine and Institue Santa Monica

You can order this 300 page profusely illusttrated manual by checking with your local health food store or by calling 619-475-2874. Total Cost: $17.95. Dr. Donsbach feels this is his best work yet. You should have his book on your shelf to help you answer health questions that may come up. It is the best review of the application and merits of wholistic health philosophy available today.

If you liked this booklet, you will probably enjoy some of the other writings of these two doctors:
* Arthritis
* Candidiasis &Chronic Fatigue
* Heart Disease/Oral Chelation
* High Blood Pressure
* Allergies and Stress
* Hypoglycemia & Diabetes
* Hysterectomy & Menopause
* Oxygen Therapy ($O_2O_2O_2$)
* Water
* Wholistic Cancer Therapy
* Get Well Through Self-Detox
* Acne, Eczema, Psoriasis
* Overwieght & Underweight
* Interpreting Blood & Urine Tests
* Live Cell Therapy
* Acupressure, Bee Pollen,
* Ginseng
* Neg. Ions, Ozone & Clean Air
* Non-Invasive Testing

NERVOUS SYSTEM

The nervous system detects and interprets changes in conditions inside and outside the body and responds to them. The central nervous system analyzes information and initiates responses; the peripheral nervous system gathers information and carries the response signals. Some responses are involuntary; others are dictated by conscious thought. All nervous system activity consists of signals passed through pathways of inter-connected neurons (nerve cells).

Peripheral nervous system

This system comprises all the nerves connecting the brain and spinal cord to the rest of the body. Of these, 31 pairs (the spinal nerves) connect to the spinal cord and 12 pairs (cranial nerves) connect to the brain. The main nerves of the limbs are labeled.

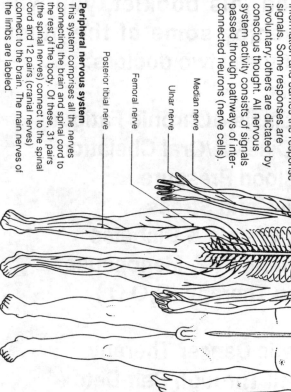

Median nerve

Ulnar nerve

Femoral nerve

Posterior tibial nerve

Brain

Brain stem

Spinal cord

Ventral root

Dorsal root

Gray matter

White matter

Vertebra

Spinal nerve

Structure of the spinal cord

The gray matter contains nerve cell bodies; white matter contains their conducting fibers. On joining the cord, spinal nerves split into two. The dorsal root carries sensory fibers; the ventral root carries motor fibers.

Central nervous system

This system consists of the brain and spinal cord, protected by the skull and spine. The CNS receives input from sense organs and receptors and sends signals to muscles and glands, via the peripheral nervous system.

HOW IT WORKS

Some possible events in response to a finger touching a hot object are shown. A receptor sends a message, via a sensory fiber, to the spinal cord. This triggers a signal that travels, via a motor fiber, back to a muscle, which contracts to move the finger. This action is called a reflex arc. Other signals pass toward the brain.

The brain

When impulses reach the cerebral cortex, pain is felt. Other activity—concerned, for example, with memorizing the painful stimulus—may also be initiated.

Cerebral cortex

Brain stem

Eye movement

Signals arriving at the brain stem may cause more action, such as the eyes moving toward the stimulus.

Nerve fibers to brain

Gray matter

Spinal cord

The signal entering the spinal cord passes to other nerve cells by separate connections.

Motor fibers

Sensory fibers

Motor fiber

Muscle action

Sensory receptors

Sensory fiber

Sensory and motor fibers

Although the sensory and motor fibers carry signals in opposite directions, along part of their lengths they may occupy exactly the same nerve.

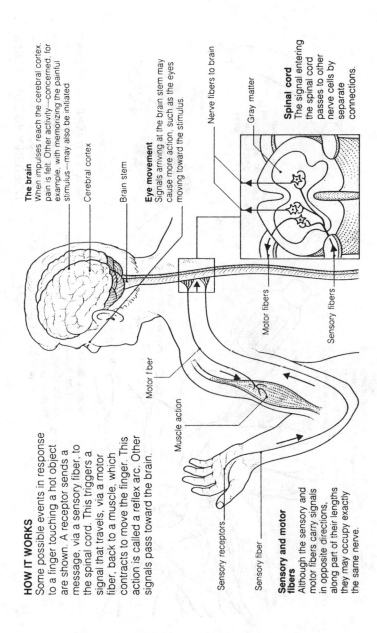

STRUCTURE OF A NEURON

A neuron (nerve cell) consists of a cell body and several branching projections called dendrites. Every neuron has a filamentous projection called an axon (nerve fiber). Axons vary in length from a fraction of an inch to several feet. An axon branches at its end to form terminals, via which signals are transmitted to target cells, such as the dendrites of other neurons, muscle cells, or glands. Bundles of the axons of many neurons are known as nerves or, within the brain or spinal cord, as nerve tracts or pathways.

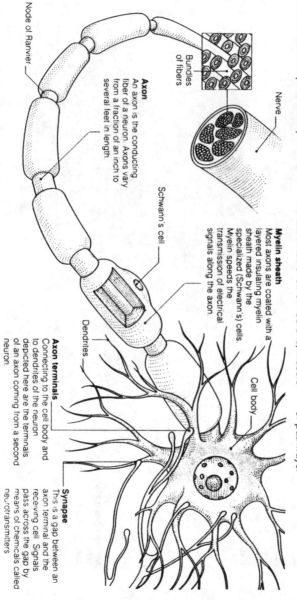

Node of Ranvier

Bundles of fibers

Nerve

Axon
An axon is the conducting fiber of a neuron. Axons vary from a fraction of an inch to several feet in length.

Schwann's cell

Myelin sheath
Most axons are coated with a layered insulating myelin sheath made by the specialized (Schwann's) cells. Myelin speeds the transmission of electrical signals along the axon.

Dendrites

Cell body

Axon terminals
Connecting to the cell body and to dendrites of the neuron depicted here are the terminals of an axon coming from a second neuron.

Synapse
This is a gap between an axon terminal and the receiving cell. Signals pass across the gap by means of chemicals called neurotransmitters.

BASIC TYPES OF NEURON

Sensory neurons carry signals from sense receptors along their axons into the CNS. Motoneurons carry signals from the CNS to muscles or glands; the axon terminals form a motor end-plate. Interneurons form all the complex interconnecting electrical circuitry within the CNS itself. For each sensory neuron in the body, there are about 10 motoneurons and 99 interneurons.

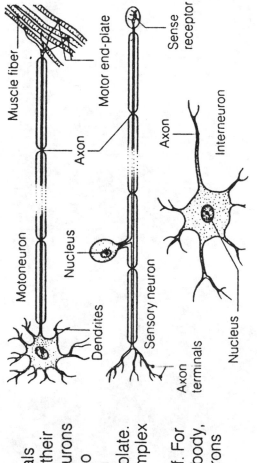